# The Step Forward

# Professional Development Program

## for Multilevel Instruction in Adult ESL Programs

**Jayme Adelson-Goldstein**

OXFORD
UNIVERSITY PRESS

198 Madison Avenue
New York, NY 10016 USA

Great Clarendon Street, Oxford OX2 6DP UK

Oxford University Press is a department of the University of Oxford.
It furthers the University's objective of excellence in research, scholarship,
and education by publishing worldwide in

Oxford  New York

Auckland  Cape Town  Dar es Salaam  Hong Kong  Karachi
Kuala Lumpur  Madrid  Melbourne  Mexico City  Nairobi
New Delhi  Shanghai  Taipei  Toronto

With offices in

Argentina  Austria  Brazil  Chile  Czech Republic  France  Greece
Guatemala  Hungary  Italy  Japan  Poland  Portugal  Singapore
South Korea  Switzerland  Thailand  Turkey  Ukraine  Vietnam

OXFORD and OXFORD ENGLISH are registered trademarks of
Oxford University Press

**Library of Congress Cataloging-in-Publication Data**

Adelson-Goldstein, Jayme.
  Step forward professional development program / Jayme Adelson-Goldstein.
    p. cm.
  ISBN 978-0-19-439877-0
  1.  English language–Study and teaching–Foreign speakers. 2.  Adult education. 3.  Effective teaching.  I. Title.
  PE1128.A2A235 2006
  428.2'4–dc22
                        2006049481

Executive Publisher: Janet Aitchison
Editorial Manager: Stephanie Karras
Assistant Editor: Carla Mavrodin
Art Director: Maj-Britt Hagsted
Senior Designer: Claudia Carlson
Production Manager: Shanta Persaud
Production Controller: Eve Wong

ISBN 978 0 19 4398770

Printed in China

10 9 8 7 6 5 4 3 2

Acknowledgments

Photo Credits: Dennis Kitchen Studio: 14, 19, 25

# Contents

# Introduction

There's something intrinsically optimistic about the act of learning. The best teachers continue their own learning by keeping up with their content areas, investigating new techniques, and, of course, learning about their learners. This professional development is key to our growth as teachers and to the growth of those we teach. Therefore it's important to seek out as many professional development opportunities as we can.

Teachers and researchers alike agree that reflective, participant-centered professional development can be a critical component in moving effective teaching strategies and techniques from theory into classroom practice. The National Center for the Study of Adult Learning and Literacy (NCSALL) published a report in 2003 entitled *How Teachers Change: A Study of Professional Development in Adult Education*. This report cites research showing that "the philosophy about professional development [has] evolved from a focus on training teachers to adopt particular, expert-recommended behaviors in the classroom to a focus on helping teachers adopt a critically reflective stance that allows them to determine for themselves what is effective."[1]

## How Will These Materials Help Me?

*The Step Forward Professional Development Program* provides opportunities for you to learn about, reflect upon, and refine your use of the teaching strategies and techniques that help you meet the varied needs of your adult ESL learners.

In addition to general student-centered instructional strategies that work across levels and programs, these materials explore the specific teaching tools you'll need to work with three types of multilevel environments. These can be described as follows:

- the so-called **single-level** class where learners fall into the categories of pre-level, on-level and higher-level learners
- the **narrow-spectrum multilevel** class where learners are formally placed into one of two or three sequential levels (e.g., a class with beginning-low and beginning-high learners, or a class with intermediate-low and intermediate-high learners).

- the **broad-spectrum multilevel** class where learners are formally placed into four or more sequential levels (e.g., beginning-low through intermediate-high learners) or placed into widely disparate levels (e.g., learners at beginning-low and intermediate-high).

While single-level classes are easier to plan for than classes that are identified as multilevel, each of these learning environments presents the same general challenge to the instructor—how to help learners with different needs and proficiency levels acquire the language and skills they need to achieve their language goals. The strategies and tools in this program will help you determine the best way to plan effective instruction for your particular teaching situation.

## How Are These Materials Arranged?

This professional development program is divided into three main sections: Getting Started, Strategies for Learner-Centered Instruction, and Mastering Multilevel Instruction.

In the Getting Started section, you'll find tips for using these materials in different professional development environments, such as study circles, peer coaching, independent study, and workshops, and for creating the teacher community so essential to real professional growth.

In the Strategies for Learner-Centered Instruction section, you'll identify and develop:

- meaningful ESL lesson objectives
- the skills that support the lesson objective
- learner-centered teaching strategies that help learners achieve the objectives

You will also work with the key elements of successful instruction. You will learn how to:

- group learners and focus them on the lesson objective
- present and process the lesson concepts
- provide guided and communicative practice
- develop daily opportunities for learners to evaluate their growth and apply what they've learned

---

[1] Smith, et al. NCSALL Report #25 November 2003 (Cambridge: Harvard Graduate School of Education), 22.

In the Mastering Multilevel Instruction section, you will find out how to:

- distinguish between different types of multilevel classes
- adapt lessons for multilevel environments
- create same and mixed-level practice activities
- identify multilevel materials that will prove effective in your classroom

Throughout each section you'll find professional development tasks (Tasks) and prompts for reflection (Reflect on...) to help you apply the program's concepts to your own teaching situation. To make this process more effective, consider starting a teaching journal (something as simple as a spiral-bound notebook will do) where you can keep track of your reflections and ideas as you work through this program.

## A Word from the Author

Some of the most intellectually exciting moments in my professional life have been spent examining ideas about teaching with ESL colleagues—learning from and teaching each other in the process. In a world where the balance is usually tilted towards "doing", taking the time to think about and discuss research, strategies, and techniques with fellow teachers is almost a guilty pleasure. My desire to refine my teaching and facilitation skills increases when I hear what other people think about ESL instruction and how they handle the same teaching issues I face. While I've found it a little nerve-wracking (in the same way bungee jumping is a little risky) to sit with colleagues and present my take on a teaching point, there's also a thrill (again, that bungee jumping analogy) in sending my ideas out in public and listening to the response. Each time I've engaged in one of these professional development excursions, I have found that my colleagues and I were anxious to try out what we'd talked about and then go forth and learn some more.

It is my sincere hope that these pages are a catalyst for similar types of experiences in your professional life. I invite you to discuss the ideas in these materials with your colleagues, try them out in your class, and then go forth and learn some more!

Jayme Adelson-Goldstein

*The Step Forward Professional Development Program* can be used for independent study, as part of a study circle, as a peer coaching or mentoring opportunity, or as the foundation for a workshop series. If you haven't already, you may want to share these materials with your coordinator to see if there are other instructors who would be interested in pursuing professional development on multilevel instruction.

## Ways to Pursue Professional Development

**Independent Study:** The first step in conducting effective independent learning is for you to set your own goals for the process. After determining your own professional development goals, identify the materials in this program that will help you achieve them. Keeping a teaching journal to record your thoughts throughout the process is highly recommended—writing your ideas and questions about these materials and your classroom experiences will help you focus on your progress towards your goals.

**Study Circles:** To use these materials as a study circle tool, first look through the materials as a group and determine the best way to divide them up, making a schedule of which readings and tasks need to be completed by which meeting. It's best to allow at least a week between study circle meetings in order for everyone to have time to read the materials, complete the assigned task(s), apply the new information to the classroom, and reflect on the results. While study circle members usually determine the discussion topics based on their interactions with the reading material and their classroom experiences, the prompts for reflection that appear throughout this program can serve as additional avenues for discussion.

**Peer Coaching:** In peer coaching, colleagues take turns identifying areas where they want to refine their instruction, observing each other teach, and meeting to plan and support instructional change. Once you and your colleagues have identified your goals for the peer-coaching process, you can select from the readings and tasks in these materials to determine how to proceed.

| Reflect On... | Answer the following questions in your teaching journal: |
|---|---|
| *the Professional Development Process* | *What are my personal professional development goals? How can I make the process work best for me? What, if any, obstacles will I need to overcome? How will I manage these obstacles?* |

## Creating a Community of Teachers

However you choose to use this program, the professional development process will be far more meaningful if, after applying the strategies, tasks, and activities from these pages to your own classroom, you then discuss the results with one or more colleagues. While we know that creating a community of teaching colleagues allows us to bring a richer level of experience to our classroom instruction, it can be a challenge to find the time to network. Here are a few ways to jumpstart this type of community building.

For teachers working at a school site:

- Before class, while working at the copy machine or office counter, take the opportunity to casually ask a general teaching question of the teachers in the room (e.g., *How do you handle error correction? Where do you find visuals?*) It is probably better not to ask a direct question about a colleague's lesson until trust has been established.

- Set up a time to exchange successful classroom activities. Plan a "swap shop" where you and your colleagues select favorite activities and then duplicate and exchange copies of the activity worksheets during a class break. Another way to share ideas is to post a favorite activity sheet and an index card with a brief description of the activity on a bulletin board or wall in the teacher's workroom.

- Encourage one or more of your colleagues to attend a state or regional TESOL conference with you. Gather new ideas to bring back to your site and share.

For teachers working in branch locations:

- Look into the possibility of having quarterly meetings where all branch teachers can exchange ideas and problem-solve the challenges at their locations.
- Partner with a colleague who is teaching students at the same level. Check in with one another on a regular basis to discuss successes and challenges in the classroom.
- Use state, regional and international TESOL organizations' listservs and websites to interact with colleagues in your area, throughout the U.S. and overseas.

You will find the exchange of ideas and the support that a teaching community affords invaluable. Once you have identified and connected with colleagues who are as interested in the process of teaching as you are, your teaching life will be profoundly affected by your awareness of, and confidence in, your instructional choices.

## Task: Create a teacher community.

Select one of the ideas above or come up with your own idea for building community with your fellow teachers. Act on one of these ideas within the next week.

### Identifying Your Professional Development Needs

In order to plan instruction it is critical to assess what students already know and what they want to know. It is no less critical for us to assess ourselves along these lines in order to make the professional development process meaningful. Before embarking on this program, consider you own instructional needs.

## Task: Consider your professional development needs.

Use the Self-Assessment Survey on page 8 to determine which instructional strategies or activities you are already using and which you would like to use more often.

## Self-Assessment Survey

Mark each strategy, technique or activity according to how often you implement it in your class:

4 = every class    3 = often    2 = sometimes    1 = rarely    0 = never

Note: The page numbers in parentheses indicate where these lesson elements are discussed in this book.

| | Instructional Strategy, Technique, or Activity | Rating |
|---|---|---|
| 1 | Assess what learners already know about a lesson topic. (p. 9) | |
| 2 | Develop objectives that match learners' needs. (p. 11) | |
| 3 | Use Mixers, Surveys or other types of low-stress, high-interest activities to build class community. (pp. 11, 15, 23) | |
| 4 | Present new language and information in a way that is comprehensible to all learners in the class. (p. 24) | |
| 5 | Check learners' comprehension of each key concept in a lesson before moving forward. (p. 15) | |
| 6 | Teach the support skills (grammar, vocabulary, pronunciation, group management and team skills) necessary to achieve the lesson objective. (pp. 13, 24) | |
| 7 | Implement a variety of grouping strategies during a lesson (e.g. individual, pairs, small groups, large groups, whole class) (p. 15–18) | |
| 8 | Provide learner-to-learner practice activities for each key concept in a lesson. (pp. 13–14, 25) | |
| 9 | Use activities and questions that increase cross-cultural awareness and higher-level thinking at all levels. (pp. 16, 23) | |
| 10 | Incorporate a real-life communication task into the lesson. (pp. 11, 14) | |
| 11 | Assess learners' achievement of the lesson objective with a task that matches the objective's language skill. (e.g., a role play for a listening/speaking objective, a multiple choice test for a reading objective, etc.) (pp. 12, 31) | |
| 12 | Close the class with an activity that allows learners to identify what they've learned. (p. 23) | |

Look at those items you marked as 2, 1, or 0. These may be the strategies or activities that you'll want to focus on as you work with this program.

# Strategies for Learner-Centered Instruction

## Instructional Strategies

Research into second-language acquisition supports a surprising theory: teachers using very different methods can have equal levels of success. (Brinton 2005) Naturally, we still seek to find the *best* method of instruction. If we consider that our ability to help our learners achieve communicative competence in English is directly linked to our ability to work with their various backgrounds, abilities, needs, and strengths, then it makes perfect sense that meaningful instruction for *all* learners would require varying techniques and methodologies. We can help our learners and ourselves by making use of a variety of techniques, but we can also avail ourselves of strategies that apply across levels and methods. The following strategies will help you develop successful learner-centered lessons regardless of which levels you teach or which method and techniques you use:

## Strategy 1

**Assess learner needs, abilities, goals, and interests before planning instruction.**

Learner-centered instruction has moved from ideal to reality in many educational settings. Learner persistence—learners' ability to stick with an educational plan to achieve their goals—is an obvious outcome when learners see that their classroom learning relates to their own needs, goals, and interests.

Despite the existence of curricula that address the needs and goals of learners at different proficiency levels, it is still up to teachers, as the facilitators of the learner-centered environment, to identify the specific needs of their learners. Pre-assessment activities can tell you what your learners already know about the lesson topic and information-gathering activities can tell you what your learners want to know.

The following pre-assessment and information-gathering activities can help you identify your learners' needs:

- During the first week of class, ask learners to look through the illustrated topics in *The Oxford Picture Dictionary* and identify topics or concepts they want to learn about.

- Before introducing any new topic, assign learners a Round Table Label. Have small groups study a picture relating to the topic and take turns listing or labeling everything they see in the picture. Learners can do this at either the word or sentence level. Collect the pictures to discover what vocabulary and structures they already know.

Use Round Table Label activities like this one to help assess learners' prior knowledge before teaching the vocabulary or structures that support the lesson objective.
From the *Step Forward Multilevel Activity Book 2*. S Wagner. (New York: Oxford University Press 2006), 78.

- Before launching into the presentation of the target competency or grammar point, use a multiple choice test to assess learners' prior knowledge. You may choose to use a test generator which allows you to easily create customized pre- and post-tests for your classes.

- Interviews, Mixers, and Surveys, such as "Let's Talk Small Talk" below, provide structured language practice for learners while giving you insights into their goals and interests. Learners can ask and answer sets of similarly structured *Yes/No* questions, such as *Do you like to…work with your hands?…with technology?*, or ask a variety of information questions, such as *Where do you go to relax?* or *What do you do on your day off?* These activities can be done in pairs, small groups, or as a whole class. This kind of interactive practice also helps establish a participatory learning environment, which is so critical for language development.

## Let's Talk Small Talk

**1**. Read the question. Mark your answers with a check (✓).

**2**. Interview 3–9 classmates. Check your classmates' answers.

| What are your favorite small-talk topics? | My Answers | My Classmates' Answers | | | | |
|---|---|---|---|---|---|---|
| sports | | | | | | |
| weather | | | | | | |
| movies | | | | | | |
| music | | | | | | |
| television | | | | | | |
| family | | | | | | |
| school | | | | | | |

This Survey gives insight into the topics learners enjoy talking about.
from the *Step Forward Multilevel Activity Book 2*. S Wagner.
(New York: Oxford University Press 2006), 32.

## Task: Develop pre-assessment and information-gathering activities.

**Imagine that you want to find out what your learners already know and what they'd like to know about renting an apartment. Plan one activity you could use to assess their prior knowledge, and one activity you could use to discover their interests and goals.**

# Strategy 2

**Create classroom community.**

It's as important for learners to know about one another as it is for you to know about them. Our learners' primary objective is communication, and at least 50–70 percent of the communication in your class should occur among learners. While the instructor develops the welcoming and accepting ambiance of the classroom, learners need to connect with one another, not just with the teacher. In addition to Mixers and Surveys, there are numerous activities you can use to build class community. For example, Line Up activities are an effective way to take a snapshot of the class. In a Line Up, learners stand and arrange themselves based on criteria such as the spelling of their first or last name, their birthday (month and day, not year), or the number of people in their family. They then turn to the people on either side of them to ask and answer simple questions related to the Line Up topic.

One of the easiest community-building activities to prepare is a Corners activity. Corners can be used to discover learners' goals and interests, and can also create a "real time" class profile, reflecting learners' favorite foods, colors, and so on. Begin by posting four to eight signs relating to one theme around the room. For example, to determine the class's learning activity preferences, you could post signs that say *Work with a partner, Work with a group, Work alone,* and *Work with the teacher*. Model the activity by walking to the corner that represents your learning preference. Then set a 30-second time limit for learners to choose and go to a corner. There, learners can introduce themselves to the other people in the same corner. Higher-level learners can state why they chose the corner. You can extend the activity by asking learners to go to the corner that represents their least favorite choice.

## Task: Develop community-building activities.

**Imagine your goal is to build class community and to find out where your learners use English.**

- Write five *Yes/No* Mixer questions learners could ask each other on this topic.
- Prepare four to six Corners signs that would work for this topic.

# Strategy 3

**Plan instruction around an objective that identifies what learners will be able to do by the end of the lesson.**

Research shows that adult learners want to know why they're learning what they're learning. (Knowles 1973) In addition, they need to be assured that the skills and competencies they achieve in class will be applicable to their lives outside the classroom. By basing lesson objectives on learners' needs, the lesson becomes meaningful to the learner and the achievement of the lesson objective signals the achievement of a skill or competency that learners will value.

In writing lesson objectives, teachers also need to consider four elements: context, communication task, language proficiency focus, and evaluation[2]. The chart on page 12 shows how identifying each aspect of an objective will help you identify ways to plan the presentation, practice, and evaluation stages of a lesson.

Many teachers start lesson planning by identifying an objective and planning the presentation, practice, evaluation, and application activities that match that objective. Other teachers have found it helpful to start from a communication task that matches their learners' needs, deriving the objective from that task. Backward lesson planning refers to building a lesson plan from the evaluation task back up through the presentation. Whichever way the lesson plan is conceived, a clearly defined objective is a determining factor in the success of the lesson.

---

[2] *An Objective Approach to Lesson Planning*, Adelson-Goldstein, J. and J. Owensby, 2004.

## Identifying Key Elements of a Lesson Objective

**Sample objective:** *Learners will be able to introduce themselves in class, ask for their classmates' names, and spell their own names.*

| To Determine: | Ask Yourself These Questions: | Example: |
|---|---|---|
| The Context | In which situation(s) will the new language be used? What's the link between the objective and learners' lives? | This context is classroom introductions, but the language could be applied to other contexts as well (e.g., a party, an interview, a date). The necessity of working with fellow classmates links this objective to the learners' lives. |
| The Communication Task | What is the communicative purpose of the lesson? (e.g., listening for information, describing an event, reading and talking about a passage, writing a note). | The purpose is to make introductions, so the communication task should revolve around students mixing and introducing themselves. |
| The Language Proficiency Focus | Does the objective focus on listening, speaking, reading, writing, or a pairing of these? | The language proficiency focus is on speaking (asking for, spelling) with a secondary focus on listening (listening for names, responding to requests to spell). |
| The Evaluation | How will achievement of the objective be evaluated? Does the evaluation match the language proficiency focus? For example, learners' speaking abilities are not tested with a paper and pencil test. | The evaluation for this objective could be a Mixer (observed by the teacher) where learners make and respond to requests to give and spell their names, writing down the correct spelling of the names they hear. |

| **Reflect On...** *Developing Lesson Objectives* | Read through the chart above and answer this question in your journal: *What roles should national standards, district curricula, textbooks, and learners' needs play in the development of lesson objectives?* |
|---|---|

# Strategy 4

**Identify the skills that support the achievement of the lesson objective.**

Accurate grammar, vocabulary use, and pronunciation play important roles in our learners' communicative competence. In the case of the sample objective in the chart on the previous page: *Learners will be able to introduce themselves in class, ask for their classmates' names, and spell their own names,* learners would need to learn the letters of the alphabet, the terms *first name, last name, ask, answer, question, spell,* and functional words such as *please*. The information question *What's your name?* could lead to a mini-presentation on how to use the verb *to be* and possessive adjectives. Learners might also need help with the pronunciation of *b, v,* and *p* while spelling.

Communication skills (e.g., active listening) and group management skills (e.g., time management) are additional support skills learners need to succeed in the classroom, the community, and the workplace. If, for example, learners are going to be evaluated on their ability to exchange information in a Mixer setting, they might need some instruction in the skills of turn-taking, clarification, and participation.

By identifying and teaching the support skills needed to achieve the lesson objective, the lesson becomes more cohesive and learners can see how it relates directly to their lives.

## Task: Identify necessary support skills.

**Select one of the objectives below or choose one of your own. Identify the key elements of the objective and the support skills learners would need in order to achieve the objective.**

• Learners will be able to respond to basic job interview questions.

• Learners will be able to identify local, state, and federal government leaders.

• Learners will be able to interpret a housing ad.

# Strategy 5

**Provide more learner-to-learner talk time (practice) than teacher-talk time (presentation).**

When learners have limited language to work with, it can be very tempting for any instructor to stand front and center for much of the lesson, taking the class quickly through the lesson materials. Learners need time to work with the new language, and they also need time to synthesize it with their previously acquired language. Of course, we want to provide engaging presentations and check our learners' comprehension before moving on to practice activities, but we also want to be sure that presentations are brief enough for learners to be able to remember what they've learned while they practice and apply it.

The presentation/practice balance can be a tricky one for classes with learners at the pre-production stage of language development. In the first weeks of a low-level class, it may be necessary for a greater percentage of practice time to be taken up by learners responding to the teacher's commands. As soon as possible, however, learners should begin working with peers in interactive and communicative practice activities.

The practice stage of the lesson is the easiest period in which to manage learner-to-learner talk time. Practice activities generally fall into two categories: guided (or more controlled practice) and communicative (or less controlled practice). In a guided practice activity, the learners are working with materials and structures that will support accurate production of the new language. In addition to whole-class drills and independent workbook activities, guided practice can also be highly interactive. One highly interactive guided practice activity that works with learners at any level is a peer dictation.

In a Peer Dictation, pairs take turns dictating letters of the alphabet, numbers, target words and phrases, or sentences and questions to each other. Dictating helps learners focus on accurate pronunciation, grammar, vocabulary use, and lesson content. It also encourages them to employ useful clarification strategies. In listening to each other, they will most likely need to request the spelling or repetition of an item. Explicitly teaching a target clarification strategy, such as *How many? Who? Put it where?*, before learners work together, is critical to the success of this activity.

During a communicative practice activity, the focus is on fluency rather than accuracy. Once learners have prepared themselves with the guided practice activities, they're ready to complete a communication task that uses what they've learned but also makes use of their prior knowledge and has an element of the unknown. Examples of these types of tasks include Grid Games (see below), a jigsaw (or paired) reading activity, a role play, or a team project such as creating a poster or booklet together. These types of activities reinforce and expand learners' use of the language.

In a Grid Game, partners tell each other where to place picture cards on their grids to end up with matching grids. See the *Step Forward Step-By-Step Lesson Plans* for other ways to increase learner-to-learner talk time.

| **Reflect On...** *Balancing Learner and Teacher Talk Time* | Think about a recent class you taught or participated in and answer the following questions in your journal: *What percentage of the class time was spent in learner-to-learner communication? What percentage of the time was teacher talk? Was the balance right for the class? How might it have been adjusted?* |
|---|---|

# Managing Groups

While the five basic strategies just presented are the foundation of learner-centered instruction, their use does not automatically create a learner-centered environment. We know that learner-to-learner interaction in pairs and small groups is a critical component of any language lesson and that these practice activities bridge the gap between the presentation of the new information and its application in the world outside the classroom. Some of our learners, however, strongly believe in a teacher-centered classroom. This is usually the basis for the resistance we face when we try to turn the focus away from teacher-to-learner presentation towards learner-to-learner communication. The following tips will enable you to use pair and group activities more successfully in your classroom:

- Create class community. The better learners know and respect each other, the more likely they are to work well together. Point out that working with peers creates a more authentic exchange than listening to a teacher in front of a class.

- Avoid the confusion that ensues when learners are put into pairs or groups before they're ready to use the language. Start out the practice stage of your lesson with very guided activities that give learners a safe environment to try out the new language. Have learners repeat language or answer questions chorally. For literate learners, provide time to copy new words, sentences, questions, or grammar structures in their notebooks.

- Use perimeter activities such as Corners, Line Ups, and Mixers to combat the resistance to move from one seat to another for group activities. Ask learners to meet up in groups or pairs along the walls or in the front or back of the class. They can work in a neutral part of the class and then move back into their own seats when the activity is over.

- Use Mixers that randomly pair people to help learners benefit from working with someone other than a best friend or spouse. Try giving one half of the room one color card and the other half a different color card, then ask learners to meet someone whose card is different from their own. Once learners are paired, have them introduce themselves and complete a simple task that relates to the lesson objective and/or topic.

- Manage the "speed spectrum" of group activities. (If one group has finished the activity, chances are quite good that another group hasn't quite gotten started and another group is about half-way through). Set time limits to help learners stay on task. Let learners know when time is up, but then ask if more time is needed. Set a new time limit for the groups that need more time and give groups that have finished with Keep Going activities.

- Give specific tasks to learners who would normally dominate a group. If the "dominator" is a higher-level student, give him or her the task of asking follow up questions to groups who finish early.

- Follow these steps to avoid the "translation imperative"—where learners immediately ask each other (in their first language) *What do we do?* as soon as you start an activity:

1) Explain the activity simply, giving the goal and reason for doing the activity and using visuals to support your language when possible.

2) Review the activity worksheet on the overhead and check vocabulary comprehension.

3) Model or demonstrate the activity to learners.

4) Check comprehension by asking *Yes/No* and information questions. Encourage learners to restate the steps of the activity to their partner or group.

---

**Reflect On...**
*The Challenges Learners and Teachers Face*

Think about the different challenges to managing group work effectively and answer these questions in your journal:
*Which challenges have you experienced? How did you handle them?*
*What do you think your learners find most challenging about working with other learners? Why? What are some ways that you could help them overcome these challenges?*

## Teaching Communication and Group Management Skills

Before learners can successfully work together, they need to practice the skills they will need in their group work, such as checking information, giving feedback, disagreeing, restating, managing time, keeping the group on task, encouraging each other, participating, listening actively, etc.

The *Do/Say* chart, a cooperative learning tool, provides explicit instruction in these types of skills. On a piece of poster board, a tearsheet, or butcher paper, write the focus skill at the top of the page and make two columns: one for things you do and one for things you say when you demonstrate the skill. See the example below.

| To Listen Actively You Can... | |
|---|---|
| Do This | Say This |
| lean forward | Yes, I see. |

from Kagan, Spencer. *Cooperative Learning*. San Clemente, (CA: Kagan Publishing, 1994) 14:7–8.

Depending on your learners' proficiency level(s), you can elicit examples for each column from the class or simply demonstrate and write examples on the chart. Once you have four or more examples in each column, pair learners and have them practice acting out each of the examples. This is a key part of the process. While it often generates laughter, it ensures that learners get a chance to practice the language and behaviors associated with the skill before they're asked to put it to use. Once learners are in groups or pairs, encourage them to use the communication or group management skill that you've taught. Refer learners to the chart throughout the week. Whenever summing up your observations about learners' work during a group activity, be sure to praise learners who have used the target behaviors and language during the activity.

**Task:** Create a *Do/Say* chart for a communication or group management skill.

a. Imagine you want your learners to practice active listening during a group task. One behavior you could demonstrate would be leaning forward. Make a *Do/Say* chart of at least three other behaviors and three expressions that active listeners use.

b. Select one of the skills from the list below and create a *Do/Say* chart for that skill:

- Taking turns
- Encouraging classmates
- Working with time limits
- Getting clarification

## Techniques for Grouping Learners

How you group your learners depends on which activities have been planned and where they occur within the lesson. The following techniques for getting learners into groups may make the process easier:

- Give different colored dots, index cards, or folders to learners in different areas in the classroom. You can then tell learners to find someone with a dot (card, folder) of a different color. To create groups of four, have each pair join another pair. (You can also distribute one color to weaker learners and the other color to stronger learners so that when they pair, higher-level learners will be in a position to help their classmates).

- Assign each student a letter (A, B, C) as they enter the classroom, and then use those letters to create groups. Learners can look for someone with the same letter or a different letter.
- Duplicate A/B paired activity worksheets on different colored paper and tell learners to find someone with a different color sheet.
- Prepare a set of group signs, each with 4–6 different learners' names on them and place them around the room or on tables before learners arrive. As they enter the room, direct them to look for their group and introduce themselves.
- Count off to create small groups. First divide the number of learners by the number of people you want in each group (e.g., to make groups of four in a class of 30 learners, divide 30 by 4 to get 7 with a remainder of 2. Then have the learners count off from 1–7. Go around the room until everyone has a number. The last two learners in the room will be #1 and #2 respectively). Ask all the #1s to get up and form a group, all the #2s, #3s etc. (Note that both the #1s and #2s will have five people in their groups).

## Task: Create and manage groups.

**Examine the activities from the textbook on page 18 (or use activities from a lesson in your textbook) in order to determine the following:**

1) How are learners grouped in each activity?

2) Is this the way you would choose to group learners? Why or why not?

3) How would you get learners into groups or pairs for these activities?

4) How would you help learners buy in to these activities?

5) Which communicative or group work skills would learners need to be successful with these activities?

# Sample Activities from a Textbook

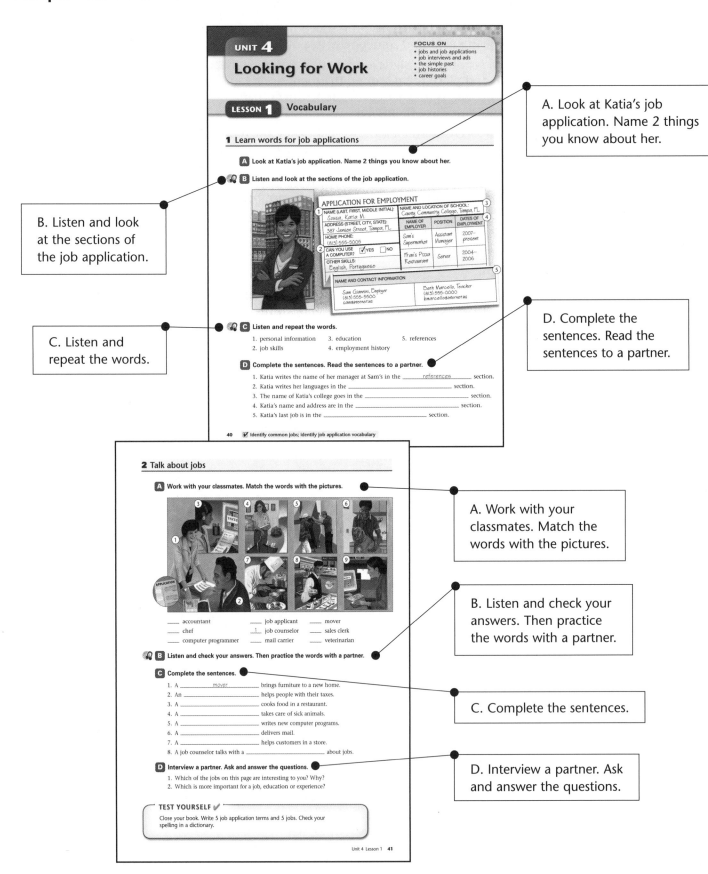

A. Look at Katia's job application. Name 2 things you know about her.

B. Listen and look at the sections of the job application.

C. Listen and repeat the words.

D. Complete the sentences. Read the sentences to a partner.

A. Work with your classmates. Match the words with the pictures.

B. Listen and check your answers. Then practice the words with a partner.

C. Complete the sentences.

D. Interview a partner. Ask and answer the questions.

from *Step Forward Book 2*. I. Wisniewska,
(New York: Oxford University Press, 2007), 40–41.

# Mastering Multilevel Instruction

## Distinguishing Between Multilevel Classes

In a general sense, multilevel means so much more than differentiating between ability levels—it encompasses differences in background, interest, learning style, intelligence, economic status, age, and gender. These differences make it imperative that lessons meet a range of learners' needs, abilities, and goals.

There are three basic types of multilevel environments: single-level with level variations, narrow-spectrum classes with two or three levels in sequence, and broad-spectrum classes with four or more levels or non-sequential levels. See the chart on page 20 for examples of these environments and how learners may be grouped within them.

Whether you're teaching in a single-level setting with slight differences between learners' needs and abilities, or in an identified multilevel class with even greater differences between learners' levels and skills, you know the benefits of having a varied learner population:

- Variety in the class community creates an interesting and energized atmosphere.

- Learners can work on different language proficiencies at different levels (e.g., an intermediate-level writer with beginning-level speaking skills can receive targeted instruction in both skill areas).

- Higher-level learners serve as role models and are able to model language for lower-level learners.

- Lower-level learners who are exposed to language above their level often learn more than learners who only work with their same-ability group.

These and other benefits help to balance the challenges of teaching a multilevel class.

---

**Reflect On...**
*The Benefits of the Multilevel Classroom*

Think about the benefits mentioned in this section and answer these questions in your journal: *What is the single greatest benefit for learners in a multilevel classroom? For teachers? For a school program? What other benefits result from multilevel instruction?*

---

In this narrow spectrum multilevel class, learners are preparing a role play set in the waiting room at a clinic. When the group presents the role play, learners in the audience will listen for specific information appropriate to their levels. (e.g., beginning-low learners will listen for the patient's complaint, beginning-high learners will listen for the clerk's directions, and intermediate-low learners will evaluate their classmates' pronunciation, accuracy and creativity).

# Three Types of Multilevel Environments

## Single-level Class With Level Variations

| Possible Proficiency Groups for a Beginning-low Class | |
|---|---|
| **Proficiency Group** | **Description** |
| Pre-level | Learners with low literacy skills or students who entered the class mid-way into the semester or quarter. |
| On-level | Learners who placed at beginning-low. |
| Higher-level | Learners who placed into beginning-low and either tested lower than their actual skills or who have a beginning-high proficiency in one or two skill areas. |

## Narrow-Spectrum Multilevel Class with 2 or 3 Sequential Levels

| Possible Proficiency Groups for a class with Pre-Literacy, Beginning-low and Beginning-high learners | |
|---|---|
| **Proficiency Group** | **Description** |
| Lower-level | Learners who placed at the pre-literacy level. |
| Mid-level | Learners who placed at the beginning-low level. |
| Higher-level | Learners who placed at the beginning-high level. |

## Broad-Spectrum Multilevel Class with 4+ or non-Sequential Levels

| Possible Proficiency Groups for a Class with Literacy through Advanced-Low Learners | | |
|---|---|---|
| **Proficiency Group** | **Description** | |
| | **Reading/Writing Lessons** | **Speaking/Listening Lessons** |
| Lower-level | Learners who placed at the literacy level. | Learners who placed at the literacy and beginning-low levels. |
| Mid-level | Learners who placed at beginning-low and beginning-high levels. | Learners who placed at the beginning-high and intermediate-low levels. |
| Higher-level | Learners who placed at intermediate to advanced levels. | Learners who placed at intermediate-high to advanced-low levels. |

# Multilevel Strategies

The body of research on multilevel instruction includes numerous references to the work published by Bell (1991), Terrill and Shanks (1995), Hess (2001), and the ESL Teacher Institute training materials developed by Hampson and Knight-Mendelson and revised by CALPRO (2004). Each of these materials focuses on similar sets of strategies that lead to successful multilevel instruction. The seven following strategies work equally well with single-level variations, narrow-spectrum, and broad-spectrum multilevel classes.

## Multilevel Strategy 1

**Identify three ability groups in a class to aid instructional planning.**

Once learners' needs have been assessed (see page 9), it is helpful to create three basic proficiency groups. In classes where learners are not formally identified as being at different levels, it may be helpful to think of these three groups as pre-level, on-level, and higher-level. For classes with learners enrolled at different levels you could label the groups lower-level, mid-level and higher-level (or even A, B and C). In a class with a broad spectrum of learners ranging from pre-literacy level to intermediate-high, the lower-level group might include both pre-lit and beginning-low learners, the mid-level group might be the beginning-high learners and the higher-level group would be the intermediate-low learners.

The membership of these groups may shift based on the proficiency focus of the lesson (e.g., a strong writer may be less skilled in speaking and so work with one group of learners on a writing task and another group of learners on a speaking task). Even in classes where there are four or more distinct levels, creating three general groups will help facilitate instruction and learner interaction by allowing teachers to plan learning activities to match the proficiencies of their learners.

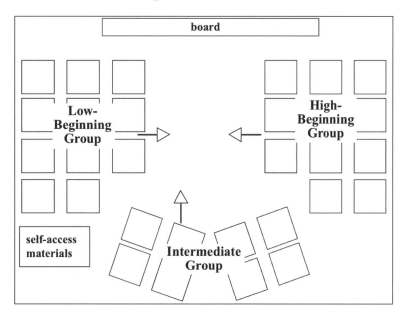

An example of grouping in a class with tab arm desks. Arrows indicate learners' visual orientation.

**Reflect On...**
*Grouping by Proficiency*

Think about and answer the following questions in your teaching journal:
*What are some benefits and drawbacks of grouping learners by level within a class?*
*How can instructors keep track of group affiliations if learners move in and out of groups depending on the lesson proficiency focus?*

# Multilevel Strategy 2

**Plan lessons around a single theme or topic then identify level-specific objectives.**

After assessing your learners' needs and comparing those needs to your course curriculum, as well as to state and federal standards, lesson planning can be simplified by looking at themes or general topics that work across levels. *Shopping for Clothing, Eating Well,* and *Seeking Medical Treatment* are examples of topics that would be meaningful for learners at all levels. Once a topic has been identified for a lesson, the teacher determines the language needs within that topic for each of the three identified proficiency groups and creates three level-specific lesson objectives.

Imagine, for example, that you are teaching a narrow-spectrum multilevel class with beginning-low, beginning-high, and intermediate-low learners. The topic is clothing, and for one lesson you've created the following three objectives:

- Beginning-low learners will be able to identify 8–10 clothing items by color and price.
- Beginning-high learners will be able to ask for a clothing item by color and size.
- Intermediate-low learners will be able to return a clothing item and request an exchange for another size or color.

In this class, the beginning-low learners will be exposed to language that supports all three objectives, but only held accountable for achieving their level objective. The beginning-high and intermediate-low learners will benefit from the review inherent in the presentation of the beginning-low material, and incorporate that material as they work to achieve their own level objectives.

## Task: Create multilevel objectives.

**Imagine that you've taught the lesson above and are now planning the next day's lesson. Your mid-level objective is "Learners will be able to interpret common clothing care labels." Develop two parallel objectives for your lesson, one for the lower-level group and one for the higher-level group.**

# Multilevel Strategy 3

**Begin and end each class session with a whole-class activity to build class community.**

The success of the multilevel class depends on learners' ability to work together in mixed-level groups. It's critical to establish from the outset that *all* learners, no matter what their proficiency level, contribute to the language-learning process.

Begin the class with a community-building warm-up activity that involves all learners. Later, close the class with an activity that brings the class back together to recognize the value of what they've done. During these types of activities, learners identify what they've learned during the lesson or evaluate how well the class went that day. One way to do this is to pose the question *What did we work on today?* to the whole class and elicit responses. Promote the idea that learners can and have learned from each other.

## Task: Create a closing activity.

**List three or more ways learners could share what they learned or how they felt about the lesson with you and their classmates.**

# Multilevel Strategy 4

**Present new information to the whole class at one time.**

A whole-class presentation in a multilevel class has to be comprehensible to the lower-level learners and yet challenging enough for the higher-level learners. Learners at all levels can usually understand more than they can produce, but using visuals, realia, demonstrations, repetition, and the occasional translation of a word or phrase, ensures that lower-level learners can get the gist of higher-level material. During the portions of a whole-class presentation that are review for higher-level learners, these learners can be engaged by more complex level-appropriate prompts and questions from the instructor. Those same learners can also model language that is new to other learners.

It may be helpful to conduct a mini-presentation to one level when a grammar point or vocabulary set is either too basic or too complex to be presented across levels. That said, one of the benefits of the multilevel environment is that lower-level learners are exposed to more language than they otherwise would be if they were in a regular class. They can usually rise to the challenge of listening to a contextualized presentation of a higher-level grammar point, as long as they're not asked to produce the new form. Once higher-level learners have begun practicing the new form in their same-level group, it's often possible to draw out one element from the higher-level grammar point for lower-level learners to work on (e.g., after being exposed to the future tense in a presentation on making plans using the future conditional *If I don't have to work on Saturday, I'll go to the beach*, lower-level learners can work with future tense statements about weekend plans, such as *I'll go to the beach on Saturday*).

Note, however, that in situations where one level group needs to learn material that would be irrelevant to other levels, it's best to make a separate mini-presentation to that group. For example, to achieve their objective of being able to interpret an apartment lease, higher-level learners might need an explicit presentation on active vs. passive voice (*The security deposit will not be returned in the following cases...*) The teacher would teach this form while mid- and lower-level learners were engaged in practice activities that related to the general presentation on renting an apartment.

Another technique for matching all learners' needs during a whole-class presentation is to follow the presentation by directing different types of questions to each level. For example, the following questions might be directed to learners after a presentation on shopping for clothing:

For pre-level learners, *Point to the red shirt. Is this a red shirt?*

For on-level learners, *Is this a red shirt or a red skirt? What color is the shirt? How much is the skirt?*

For higher-level learners, *What kind of shirt does she want? Does she need a receipt to exchange it?*

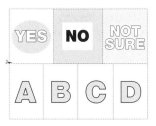

Using index cards makes it easier to identify learners' responses at a glance.

One of the pitfalls of asking questions in the multilevel class is that higher-level learners will often answer before lower-level learners can get a word in. Avert this with the use of answer cards, which allow you to check the comprehension of all learners. In response to your *Yes/No* questions, learners silently hold up a "yes", "no", or "not sure" card. You can further challenge higher-level learners by using a *Yes/No* question with a complex structure (e.g., *Would the shirt be less expensive than the skirt if they both went on sale for half price?*)

## Task: Write directed questions.

Imagine you're presenting information on prescription labels. Look at a prescription label and write 5 simple *Yes/No* questions and 5 more complex *Yes/No* questions about the information on the label.

# Multilevel Strategy 5

Use same-level[3] grouping to provide guided practice for learners.

Grouping learners in same-level groups ensures that they get the processing and practice time they need to achieve their level objective. As mentioned earlier, practice activities that can work on more than one level are very valuable in the multilevel class. One example would be a Total Physical Response activity in which same-level pairs take turns giving and acting out commands. In the classroom, pre- or lower-level learners in one area of the room would listen and respond to your commands, on- or mid-level pairs in another area of the room would take turns using written commands or picture prompts to command each other, and higher-level pairs would work with commands or create new commands at a higher language level.

When learners work autonomously in same-level groups, it's a great opportunity for you to facilitate and observe learners' level of accuracy, their use of the grammar and vocabulary that support the objective, and their pronunciation of target language.

## Task: Create same-level practice activities.

**Imagine that you are teaching a class on making a doctor's appointment. Identify different ways you could adapt a picture and conversation on this subject to serve as the basis for each of your three groups' same-level practice.**

# Multilevel Strategy 6

Use mixed-level[4] group activities to provide learners with communicative practice and fluency building.

Putting learners in mixed-level groups creates opportunities for them to apply new language in communicative practice activities that build fluency. By working in this type of group, pre-level learners often challenge themselves, and higher-level learners reinforce their learning by facilitating learning for others.

An example of this phenomenon can be seen in a mixed-level peer dictation, the "teacher" role typically goes to the higher-level learner and the "student" role goes to the lower-level learner. By design, the higher-level learner practices pronunciation, while the lower-level learner practices listening and clarification. Many activities can be adjusted this way, assigning roles or tasks to be sure that all learners can participate and succeed.

## Task: Plan mixed-level activities.

**Imagine you are planning mixed-level practice activities for the health lesson on making a doctor's appointment. Which of the following activities would you choose for your learners? Why?**

- Peer Dictation: Learners dictate sentences to each other (e.g., *Can you come in at 4?)*

- Focused Listening: Learners listen to a receptionist and patient negotiate an appointment time.

- Role Play: Learners write and act out conversations about making an appointment.

- Team Project: Learners work in groups to create a pamphlet with contact information on clinics, doctors, dentists, and other health professionals.

---

[3.] Groups of learners at the same proficiency level are also referred to as like-ability groups.
[4.] Groups where learners of different abilities work together are also called cross-ability or different-ability groups.

# Multilevel Strategy 7

Establish the learners' role in classroom and group management right from the start.

The nature of the multilevel classroom requires that learners take a very active role in classroom procedures. For example, when learners handle the distribution, collection, and storage of materials, the teacher can pay more attention to facilitating instruction.

Team tasks or projects require learners to work together to achieve a common goal. By sharing resources and ideas in mixed-level groups, learners gain valuable cooperative, group management and communication skills that can be applied in the workplace, community, and within the family.

The team project allows for maximum learner involvement and choice in the learning process. Team members choose roles that best meet their abilities and goals.

In addition, during group work, learners need to take on roles to ensure the successful completion of the group task. Posting a chart with the following roles provides you with an instant reference each time you group learners.

| ROLE | TASK |
| --- | --- |
| Leader | Read the directions or questions to your group. Help your group work together. |
| Timekeeper | Watch the time. Give your group a 1-minute warning. |
| Supplier | Get the supplies for the activity. Collect the supplies when the activity is over. |
| Recorder | Write the group's ideas. Write neatly. |
| Reporter | Tell or show the class your group's ideas. |
| Researcher | Look up words in the dictionary or look for information online. |
| Language Monitor | Remind everyone to speak English. |
| Artist | Draw your group's ideas or look for pictures online or in magazines. |

When assigning roles to learners, it may be easier for the group to have a higher-level learner take the roles of recorder and reporter, but it is possible for lower-level learners to be group leaders as long as they are provided with the language they'll need to run the group well. (See the section on *Do/Say* charts, p. 16)

**Reflect On...**
*Multilevel Strategies
1–7*

Think about and answer these questions in your teaching journal:
*Which of these strategies could be useful no matter which type of class you were teaching? Why?*
*Which multilevel strategies have you already applied in your classes? Which would you like to try?*

# Materials Selection for the Multilevel Classroom

While there are numerous published materials that can be used to support language learning, the challenge for multilevel instructors lies in finding materials that will work across levels, providing meaningful language practice for *all* learners. With storage space often at a premium and budgets always a consideration, materials need to give us the most value for the cost. The following materials can be used in myriad ways and for a variety of purposes:

- Picture dictionaries
- Picture cards
- Magazine illustrations or photos
- Audio programs (CD or cassette)
- DVDs and videocassettes
- Short readings (one-quarter page to one page)
- Real-life reading materials such as forms, ads, menus, labels, etc.
- Realia such as play money, plastic food, plastic tableware, clothing, etc.
- Reproducible worksheets

## Using Visuals and Realia

Because pictures make it possible to provide comprehensible input for lower-level learners while still challenging higher-level learners, items like picture dictionaries, picture cards, and photo or picture files are very useful in multilevel classes. Apart from these excellent resources, DVDs and video cassettes of movies, movie previews, TV clips, commercials, or newscasts can also provide the basis for activities that support each level's learning objective. In a lesson where learners are working on objectives related to talking about the weather, for example, showing a short clip from a local station's weather report can first serve as an introduction to the topic, then be replayed as presentation of new vocabulary, and used again as a guided practice activity where learners use the visual to respond to questions that match their particular objective (e.g., pre-level learners watch the screen for temperatures, on-level learners identify weather conditions on the weather map, and higher-level learners listen and watch for details on the weather and the reporters' commentaries). Learners benefit from multiple encounters with the same language within a lesson, as long as they are approaching the language in a variety of ways (e.g., listening to it, reading it, naming it, manipulating it).

Realia can also be very helpful in the multilevel class. Pre-level learners can demonstrate comprehension non-verbally by manipulating the realia, and on-level and higher-level learners can then respond to questions about the demonstration. The following is an example of a conversation based on a demonstration:

**Teacher:** Pick up the stapler, Ramon. [Ramon picks it up]
**Teacher:** Lia, did Ramon pick up the stapler or the eraser?
**Lia:** the stapler
**Teacher:** Yes. Right. Jung, tell me again. What did Ramon do?
**Jung:** He picked up the stapler.

---

**Reflect On...**
*Reusing Materials*

Imagine you are taking a language class. The teacher shows you a set of pictures as part of the lesson presentation, then asks you to work with those pictures in two different practice activities—a sequencing activity and a writing activity. Answer these questions in your journal:
*Would you be bored using the same materials throughout the lesson? Why or why not?*

---

## Using Audio Programs

Audio programs and reproducible worksheets are also essential tools for multilevel practice activities. You can play a listening passage from an ESL audio program or teacher-made recording while having each level perform a different task to demonstrate comprehension. For example, in listening to a conversation between a server and a customer, lower-level learners could listen and hold up the appropriate food picture card each time that food is mentioned, mid-level learners could copy a set of food words from the board and then circle the ones they hear in the passage, and higher-level learners could actually take down the customer's order.

Another way to handle listening practice is to give all learners a preliminary task (e.g., Listen and fill in a form with the words you hear). Before you replay the passage for a second listening, identify those learners who have completed the first task and assign them a new task for the same audio (e.g., Listen for the inferred information).

## Using Reproducible Activity Sheets

Reproducible activity books are another boon for the multilevel teacher. The combination of correction tape or liquid and the "permission to copy" make it possible to adjust a worksheet to match the skill levels of different learners in your class. The number of items on a page can be reduced, as can the amount of material learners have to write. Cutting up or only using portions of a worksheet is another way to customize materials for your class.

The worksheet shown below is an example of how learners can use the same basic material to achieve different goals. One group of learners might cut apart the pictures and sentence prompts and then match them, another group could use the worksheet as is, and a third group might be given only the pictures and asked to write imperative commands based on the pictures. Later, in mixed-level groups, all learners could take turns giving and acting out the commands based on the sentence or picture prompts.

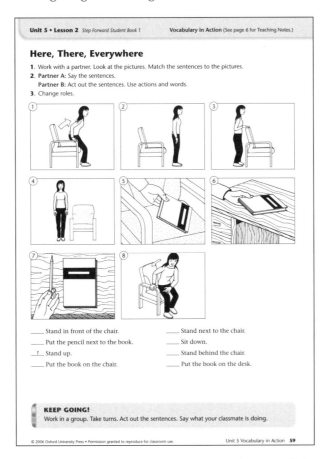

from the *Step Forward Multilevel Activity Book 1*. C. Mahdesian, (New York: Oxford University Press, 2006), 59.

## Managing the Speed Spectrum

In the multilevel class, more than any other, the speed spectrum (see p. 15) for completing tasks is wide. It is essential to have materials that learners can turn to when they have completed their group's assigned task. Self-access or "wait time" materials that take up very little space in the classroom but help learners make the most of their class time include:

• short readings with comprehension questions in a "library" file
• additional practice worksheets with answer keys
• scrambled sentences (stored in envelopes)
• vocabulary flash cards
• pictures with writing prompts

If learners have access to computers, keep a set of easy-to-follow directions for tasks, such as using a search engine to find pictures on the lesson topic, finding forms, charts, or graphs related to the topic, or using CD-ROM programs that relate to the lesson.

Perhaps the most important thing to remember about using materials in the multilevel classroom (or in any classroom for that matter) is that the materials can only be successful if learners know what they are expected to do with them. Always model the activity then follow up by checking learners' comprehension to be sure that they know what is expected of them.

## Task: Select materials for the multilevel class.

a.  **Imagine you are working with a class of beginning through intermediate-low learners on the topic of health. These are the lesson objectives:**

• Beginning-low learners will be able to tell a doctor basic symptoms.
• Beginning-high learners will be able to call and make an appointment.
• Intermediate-low learners will be able to complete a simple health history.

b.  **List the materials you would select for your whole-class presentation. Identify how you would reuse those materials in the practice stage of the lesson and list any wait time activities that would be useful for this lesson as well.**

# Using a Textbook in Multilevel Classes

Textbooks have many elements that can be utilized at different levels.

- The visuals in a text can be a source of language experience stories[5] for lower-level learners and writing prompts for higher-level learners.

- The dialogue practice can be adjusted up or down the level spectrum: pre- or lower-level learners can practice a simplified version of the conversation, on- or mid-level learners can use the prepared conversation with substitutions, and higher-level learners can close their books and try to recreate a conversation based on the one on the page.

- Grammar charts can be used to help higher-level learners puzzle out a grammar rule in small groups and lower-level learners can use them to help generate sentences to practice the grammar point.

The supplemental materials that are usually part of a textbook program, workbooks, CD-ROMs with ready-to-print practice activities, reproducible activity books, listening programs, visuals, and test generators, can also be helpful in planning same- and mixed-level practice as well as wait time activities. (See Materials Selection for the Multilevel Classroom on page 26).

| **Reflect On...** *Selecting a Textbook for a Multilevel Environment* | Rate the following elements according to which are most important for a multilevel class textbook. 1 = most important, 3 = least important |
|---|---|

____ visuals             ____ three level-specific objectives per lesson

____ realia (forms, charts, graphs)     ____ integrated skills

____ grammar charts         ____ problem solving activities

____ pair work              ____ guided practice activities

____ group work           ____ communicative practice activities

One of the most important contributions textbooks make to the multilevel class is their ability to allow learners to work autonomously. Because the directions, resources, and follow-up activities are all in one place, textbooks can facilitate assigning exercises to different groups, freeing you to observe, assist, and evaluate.

Most other textbooks correlate to just one level and are developed for use in single-level classes. If possible, select a textbook series that is designed for use in multilevel classes, such as *Step Forward* (OUP 2007). Instructors with single-level classes who want to match the needs of all their learners can go through the textbook and teacher's book in order to determine a pre-level and higher-level objective for each lesson, adjusting the textbook activities accordingly. Teachers with narrow spectrum multilevel classes can select a textbook that falls at the mid-level of the class and then write lower-level and higher-level objectives similar to the process above. Using a textbook in a broad-spectrum multilevel class usually requires selecting two or more levels of a textbook series. In classes such as these, teachers will want to select texts that mirror the broad spectrum of their learners' life skill, vocabulary, and grammar needs.

---

[5.] In learning inexperience stories, learners tell teachers, or a higher-level student, the story behind the picture or event. The teacher writes down the story, which learners are better able to read since it is in their own words.

In this type of multilevel class, the lesson plan would include the following:

- three level-specific objectives
- a whole-class warm up activity
- a whole-class presentation using visuals and/or a picture dictionary
- same-level group work in different-level textbooks
- other same-level practice activities, such as peer dictations, flash cards, and focused listening
- a mixed-level communicative practice and application activity, e.g., a team project
- a closing activity

An increased awareness of the need for materials that address multilevel instruction has led to the publication of several new books and textbooks. See the Instructional References and Resources section on page 32 for a list of textbooks and supplemental materials that support the multilevel instructional principles and strategies presented here.

## Task: Use a textbook to plan a multilevel lesson.

**Think about the low-level, mid-level, and higher-level learners in your class or imagine a class of low-beginners, high-beginners, and intermediate-low learners. Select a lesson from your current textbook (or from _Step Forward_) and take the following steps to prepare and teach a multilevel lesson for your class.**

- Identify the elements in the textbook lesson that would support multilevel instruction.
- Considering your learners' needs and using this same lesson's topic, write three sequential level-specific objectives that the textbook lesson materials could support.
- Working from the objectives above, plan a seven-stage multilevel lesson that uses some or all of the textbook lesson's materials. Plan any additional activities that learners would need to achieve their level objectives.
- Teach the lesson and reflect on what was most successful and which elements you would change.

# Challenges and Solutions in the Multilevel Classroom

While teachers of multilevel classes use some of the same strategies that are used in single-level classes, they also face challenges unique to multilevel instruction as the chart below shows.

| The Instructional Realities | The Instructional Challenge | The Instructional Solution |
|---|---|---|
| All learners want to increase their proficiency. | Learners want to work on tasks that meet their learning goals. Higher-level learners don't always want to be peer tutors, and lower-level learners want a sense of their mastery. Preparation of multiple sets of materials is not a realistic option. | Give all groups or pairs identical resources, such as pictures, worksheets, realia, etc., but assign level-specific tasks (e.g., lower-level pairs take turns showing and naming picture cards while higher-level pairs use the same picture cards as conversational prompts). |
| All learners want the teacher's attention. | Teaching exclusively to any one ability level in the class for an extended length of time can cause other levels to feel that their needs are not being met. | Have mixed-level groups work on a multilevel task. While groups are engaged, circulate and facilitate. Make a point of remarking on learners' successes. |
| All learners need to be assessed on what they've learned. | Creating multilevel performance-based assessments for speaking/listening objectives and level-specific multiple-choice tests can be daunting. | Role plays or team projects can serve as the basis for multilevel, performance-based assessment because each learner can perform at his or her own level during the task. Test generator programs now make it much easier to customize tests, so that learners can be assessed on their specific learning objectives. |
| Group work is key to multilevel instruction. | Group work often falls apart because learners aren't sure of the process or are unwilling to participate. Learners may also have difficulty managing time and resources effectively. | Assign roles to each member of a group (leader, timekeeper, recorder, reporter) and teach the language associated with those roles (e.g. *Let's start! We have one more minute. Here's what our group said*). |
| Classroom management is easier when learners are assigned to one of three proficiency levels. | A learner may work at different proficiency levels in two or more skill areas. | Provide a variety of mixed-level group tasks such as role plays where learners can self-select roles according to their ability. |
| Instructional materials must work across several levels in multilevel classes. | Adapting materials can require a lot of preparation time, especially when making materials for a mixed-level team task or pair work that has to be comprehensible to lower-level learners. | Materials that are visual and include kinesthetic or nonverbal tasks are accessible to lower-level learners. A single picture can become a source of a brainstormed word list, sentences, or a story. |
| Learners rarely work at the same pace. | When learners in some groups finish their tasks before other groups, they may start speaking in their first language and disrupt other groups' work. | Provide simple follow-up activities for learners who finish early (e.g., write 3–5 questions about the picture) or have a collection of self-access, "wait time" materials for learners to use while other groups to finish up (e.g., flashcards, workbooks, readings at different levels). |

# Instructional References and Resources

## Recommended Reading on Adult ESL Instruction and Techniques

Online Journal of the National Center for the Study of Adult Learning and Literacy, *Focus on Basics,* 2006, http://www.ncsall.net/index.php?id=168.

Brinton, Donna. "Teaching English: What is the Best Method?" *CATESOL News* 37 (2005): (2), 1, 3.

Knowles, M. *The Adult Learner: A Neglected Species.* (Houston: Gulf, 1973).

McCombs, B. and J.S. Whistler. *The Learner-Centered Classroom and School: Strategies for Increasing Student Motivation and Achievement.* (San Francisco: Josey-Bass Publishers,1997).

McMullin, Mary. *Teacher Training Through Video: Cooperative Learning ESL Techniques.* (Reading: Addison-Wesley, 1993).

Moss, Donna. "Teaching for Communicative Competence: Interaction in the ESOL Classroom" *Focus on Basics*, 2006, http://www.ncsall.net/index.php?id=739.

Parish, Betsy. *Teaching Adult ESL: A Practical Introduction.* (New York: McGraw Hill, 2004).

Papas, Peter. "Managing Small Group Learning" *Designs for Learning*, 1999 http://www.edteck.com/blocks/2_pages/small.htm.

Savage, K. Lynn, series ed. *Teacher Training Through Video: ESL Techniques* (White Plains: Longman Publishing, 1992).

Smith, Cristine, et. al. *How Teachers Change: A Study of Professional Development in Adult Education,* NCSALL Report #25 November 2003 (Cambridge: Harvard Graduate School of Education), 22.

## Recommended Reading on Multilevel Instruction

Balliro, Lenore. "Ideas for a Multilevel Class" *Focus on Basics*, 2006, http://www.ncsall.net/index.php?id=443.

Bell, Jill. *Teaching Multilevel Classes in ESL* (San Diego: Dominie Press, 1991).

Benson, P. and P. Voller. *Autonomy and Independence in Language Learning* (London: Longman, 1997).

Hampson, Nancy and Marilyn Knight-Mendelson. *Managing the Multilevel Classroom* CALPRO (California Adult Literacy Professional Development Project), 2004.

Hess, Natalie. *Teaching Large Multilevel Classes* (New York: Cambridge University Press, 2001).

Shank, Cathy C. and Lynda R. Terrill. "Teaching Multilevel Classes." *CAELA Digest*, 1995 http://www.cal.org/caela/esl_resources/digests/SHANK.html.

## Instructional Resources

Shapiro, Norma and Jayme Adelson-Goldstein. *The Oxford Picture Dictionary* (New York: Oxford University Press, 1998).

Adelson-Goldstein, Jayme, et al. *The Oxford Picture Dictionary Teacher's Book* (New York: Oxford University Press, 1998).

Weiss, Renee et al. *Classic Classroom Activities for The Oxford Picture Dictionary*. (New York: Oxford University Press, 1999).

Gramer, Margot. *The Basic Oxford Picture Dictionary 2nd Edition* (New York: Oxford University Press, 2003).

Templin-Imel, Garnet with Shirley Brod. *The Basic Oxford Picture Dictionary Literacy Program* (New York: Oxford University Press, 2003).

Shapiro, Norma, et al. *The Basic Oxford Picture Dictionary Teacher's Resource Book* (New York: Oxford University Press, 2003).

Adelson-Goldstein, Jayme and Norma Shapiro. *The Basic Oxford Picture Dictionary Teacher's Book* (New York: Oxford University Press, 2003).

Spigarelli, Jane. *Step Forward Book 1: Language for Everyday Life* (New York: Oxford University Press, 2007).

—Step Forward Book 3: Language for Everyday Life (New York: Oxford University Press, 2007).

Wisniewska, Ingrid. *Step Forward Book 2: Language for Everyday Life* (New York: Oxford University Press, 2007).

Denman, Barbara R. *Step Forward Book 4: Language for Everyday Life* (New York: Oxford University Press, 2007).

Currie Santamaria, Jenni. *Step Forward Step-By-Step Lesson Plans 1* (New York: Oxford University Press, 2007).

—*Step Forward Step-By-Step Lesson Plans 2* (New York: Oxford University Press, 2007).

—*Step Forward Step-By-Step Lesson Plans 3* (New York: Oxford University Press, 2007).

—*Step Forward Step-By-Step Lesson Plans 4* (New York: Oxford University Press, 2007).

Mahdesian, Chris. *Step Forward Multilevel Activity Book 1* (New York: Oxford University Press, 2006).

—*Step Forward Multilevel Activity Book 4* (New York: Oxford University Press, 2007).

Wagner, Sandy. *Step Forward Multilevel Activity Book 2* (New York: Oxford University Press, 2006).

Korey O'Sullivan, Jill. *Step Forward Multilevel Activity Book 3* (New York: Oxford University Press, 2007).

Podnecky, Janet. *Step Forward Workbook 1* (New York: Oxford University Press, 2007).

Russo, Renata. *Step Forward Workbook 2* (New York: Oxford University Press, 2007).

Podnecky, Janet. *Step Forward Workbook 3* (New York: Oxford University Press, 2007).

Wanage, Lise. *Step Forward Workbook 4* (New York: Oxford University Press, 2007).